# Allah Alone We Worship

### By Umm Assad

This book belongs to

_____

This book is not intended as a replacement for seeking knowledge. The reader is advised to take full responsibility for safeguarding their knowledge and understanding of Tawheed by regularly referring to authentic sources such as the Qur'an, Sahih ahadith, studying books of Scholars and their trusted students and other than that in the matters relating to his/her religion (Islam).

ISBN-13: 978-0995760714
ISBN-10: 0995760713

| | |
|---|---|
| Author | Umm Assad Bint Jamil Mohammed |
| Illustrator | A. Revello |
| Book Design | Umm Assad Bint Jamil Mohammed |
| Editor | C. Cutting |
| Published on | 2017CE/1438H |

ummassadpublications.com

Bismillahir-Rahmanir-Raheem. Indeed, all praise is for Allah. We praise Him; we seek His help, and we seek His Forgiveness. We seek refuge with Allah from the evil of our own souls and the consequence of our actions. Whomsoever Allah guides, nobody can misguide and whomsoever Allah misguides nobody can guide. I testify that none has the right to be worshipped except Allah alone, He has no partners, and I testify that Muhammad is His slave and Messenger.

# DEDICATION

*My loving Mother and Father*
*whom I love with all my heart*
*My amazingly fast growing children*
*How I pray we'll never grow apart*
*My one and only husband*
*Who has been with me from the start*
*And all those I did not mention*
*May Allah Ta'aala bless you, wherever you all are.*

*"Ameen."*

Umm Assad

**Allah alone we worship from the moment we awake.
We get up and we praise Him and do everything for His sake.**[1]

Say, "There's no deity worthy of worship, except for Allah alone,[2] and Muhammed is His Messenger," the best man ever known.[3]

**Allah is like no other. Allah is only One.**
**He has no family or a partner, no mother or a son.**[4]

**Allah sent many messengers to all nations; mankind and jinn,**[5]
**Saying, 'Worship Allah alone and don't join partners with Him'.**[6]

**We must remember to be grateful for every single day.**[7]
**We ask Allah for love and mercy.**[8] **O Allah, don't let us go astray.**

**Allah alone we obey, with complete faith and submission.**[9]
**If we believe in Allah and the last day, we must be fair and listen.**[10]

Allah alone we seek for help. We guard all our daily prayers.[11]
We never prostrate to His creation, no one else compares.[12]

**Allah alone we call our Lord, no one can take His place.**[13]
**If we call upon anyone else, all our good deeds will go to waste.**[14]

Allah alone we call others to.[15] We remind our friends and family.
We fast the month of Ramadan and give something in charity.[16]

**We enjoin all good and forbid all evil.**[17] **Uniting upon the truth.**[18]
**Having the best of manners and being examples to the youth.**[19]

For Allah's sake alone we make hajj or migrate to a Muslim land.[20]
Putting all our trust in Him alone, accepting what He has planned.

**Allah alone is our Provider. He takes care of all our needs.**[21]
**He teaches us what is good and bad, even in the food we eat.**[22]

**Allah alone is our Protector. With His knowledge, He is near.**[23]
**He is the One who tests us. So, balance hope and fear.**[24]

**Allah alone we turn to, in the rain and thunder storm.
Do not forget His Mercy, whether weak or strong.**[25]

**Allah alone we remember in the mosque and our homes too.**[26]
**He knows when we are good or not. He Sees everything we do.**[27]

Allah alone we repent to, when we've wronged our soul.[28]
We apologise to others too and learn to have self-control.

Allah alone rewards our deeds. We seek His eternal pleasure.[29]
We help others when they need. We're not just here for leisure.[30]

**Allah alone deserves our time. A Muslim is never bored.
We keep our duty to our parents, but Allah is not ignored.**[31]

**Allah alone we turn back to, feeling humble, feeling shy.
He chose Islam as our religion and it is He we glorify.**[32]

**Allah alone forgives all sins, to whoever He decides.**
**Except for shirk, the biggest sin which no one can ever hide.**[33]

**Allah alone gives guidance. He guides us to the truth.**[34]
**We study the Quran and Sunnah so our worship will improve.**[35]

So, obey Allah and His messenger then cling onto the scholars.[36]
Inheritors of the prophets, in knowledge, belief and manners.[37]

**Allah alone we worship. We do not worship any other.**[38]
**But some people do not know that they are worshipping another.**

We worship Allah as if we see Him. Do the best that we can do.
And though we cannot see Him, know that He Sees me and you.[39]

Say, "There's no deity worthy of worship, except for Allah alone, and Muhammed is His Messenger," the best man ever known.

# Glossary

**Allah**: The Name of The One True God.
**Jannah**: Paradise.
**Ramadan**: The ninth month of the Islamic calendar of which the Muslims fast.
**Hajj**: Pilgrimage to Makkah.
**Muslim**: The one who worships Allah alone.
**Quran**: The Revelation from Allah
**Sunnah**: Teachings of the prophet
**Tawheed**: Allah is the only Lord of creation, He alone, is their provider and sustainer, Allah has Names and Attributes that none of the creation share and Allah is to be singled out for worship, alone. Tawheed is maintaining the Oneness of Allah in all the above mentioned categories. Islam makes a clear distinction between the Creator and the created.

# Endnotes

1. Quran: Surah 6, Ayah 162-163
2. Quran: Surah 3, Ayah 18
3. Quran: Surah 33, Ayah 40
4. Quran: Surah 112, Ayah 1-4
5. Quran: Surah 51, Ayah 56
6. Quran: Surah 7, Ayah 59/ Surah 35, Ayah 24-26 /Surah 4, Ayah 163-167/ Surah 73, Ayah 15
7. Quran: Surah 14, Ayah 7/ Surah 13, Ayah 16
8. Quran: Surah 30, Ayah 21
9. Quran: Surah 2, Ayah 285
10. Quran: Surah 4, Ayah 59
11. Quran: Surah 2, Ayah 153/ Surah 17, Ayah 78-79
12. Quran: Surah 41, Ayah 37
13. Quran: Surah 18, Ayah 38
14. Quran: Surah 6, Ayah 88
15. Quran: Surah 16, Ayah 125/ Surah 103
16. Quran: Surah 2, Ayah 183-185/ Surah 3, Ayah 92
17. Quran: Surah 3, Ayah 110/ Surah 103
18. Quran: Surah 3, Ayah 103
19. Quran: Surah 2, Ayah 83/ Hadith: Sahih Al-Bukhari (Vol. 8, Ch. 78, No. 56))
20. Quran: Surah 3, Ayah 96-97/ Surah 16, Ayah 41
21. Quran: Surah 20, Ayah 132
22. Quran: Surah 5, Ayah 1-5
23. Quran: Surah 2, Ayah 214/Surah 50, Ayah 16/ Surah 67, Ayah 2
24. Quran: Surah 2, Ayah 143
25. Quran: Surah 10, Ayah 22-23/ Surah 40, Ayah 60 /Surah 39, Ayah 53
26. Quran: Surah 62, Ayah 10
27. Quran: Surah 49, Ayah 18
28. Quran: Surah 11, Ayah 3/ Surah 20, Ayah 82 /Surah 66, Ayah 8
29. Quran: Surah 32, Ayah 17-20/ Surah 18, Ayah 2 /Surah 99, Ayah 6-8
30. Quran: Surah 23, Ayah 115-116
31. Quran: Surah 17, Ayah 23-24
32. Quran: Surah 5, Ayah 3/Surah 3, Ayah 19/ Hadith: Sahih Al-Bukhari (Vol 1, Ch. 2, No. 37)
33. Quran: Surah 4, Ayah 48/ Surah 39, Ayah 53
34. Quran: Surah 35, Ayah 8
35. Akhlaaqul Ulemaa (pp.42-43) of Imaam al-Aajurree
36. Quran: Surah 4, Ayah 59
37. Hadith: Sahih Al-Bukhari (Vol 1, Ch. 3, No. 10) /Sheikh Al-Fawzan [Manaahij, pg. 157]
38. Quran: Surah 109
39. Hadith: Sahih Al-Bukhari (Vol 1, Ch. 2, No.50)

*Note: For more references, please refer to authentic sources.*

# ABOUT THE AUTHOR:

Umm Assad is a writer of children's educational books and homeschool resources. In spring 2017, Umm Assad was delighted to learn that her first publication reached the top ten in children's educational books as well as Islamic books and others on Amazon and sells successfully worldwide.

Her passion for writing continues to grow as she plans to produce more children's books for many years to come.

To find out more about Umm Assad, simply visit the links below. You can also contact Umm Assad where you can also download your free 'Islamic Activity Pack' to use alongside her books:

**Websites**: ummassadpublications.com, ummassadhomeschool.com
**Twitter**: ummassadpubs
**Instagram:** ummassad.pubs
**Facebook**: ummassadpubs
**Youtube**: ummassadpublications

## ummassadpublications.com
'Take Pride in Authenticity'

Made in the USA
Middletown, DE
03 May 2021

38916624R10018